Cover-ups

things to put on yourself

A Puffin Book
Written and produced by McPhee Gribble Publishers
Illustrated by David Lancashire

About cover-ups

People have always put things on themselves – for warmth, for protection from weather or enemies, to make themselves look better than other people, or the same as their friends.

You can dress yourself up in different things to feel like another person altogether.

Make a collection of things to use. Old clothes can be painted or patched or taken apart. New clothes can be made from paper and plastic and old curtains and blankets.

Collect other things, too. Buttons and beads and curtain rings can be sewn on. Poster paints and felt pens make quick patterns.

Use a sewing machine if you can. This way you get the strongest stitch and things will last longer. But sewing by hand is often the easiest way.

Back stitch makes a strong seam. Use it for long-lasting things. Put the right sides of the material together and stitch a little in from the edge.

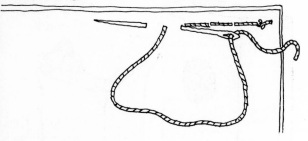

Running stitch makes quick seams and hems. Pull the thread tight for a frill.

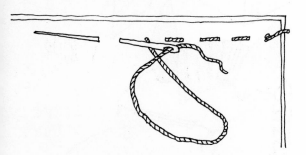

Use sticky tape and glue for joining paper. Staples and pins work for other materials, too.

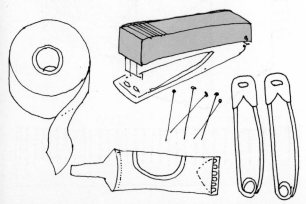

Safety pins are the quickest fastenings. A button and a loop are even better.

Use a big button and sew a loop of wool or string on the other flap of the opening.

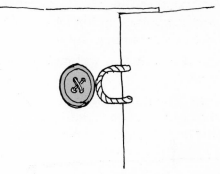

Make the loop just big enough to fit tightly over the button.

You can carve your own buttons from twigs of dry wood or pieces of pine cone. Use a penknife to cut a notch for the thread.

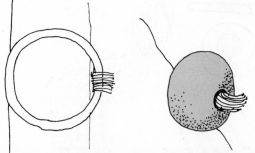

Curtain rings or fat beads can make buttons, too.

Pantomime horse

A pantomime horse looks strangely real on the stage or walking down the street.

You and a friend can be a horse together. One of you bends over and holds on to the waist of the other standing in front.

For the horse's body you will need a large square of cloth.

Cut a slit in it long enough to go round the middle of the person standing in front. Safety pins help you get a perfect fit.

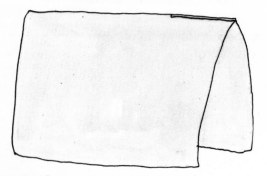

Use something that nobody wants and paint it in horse colours.

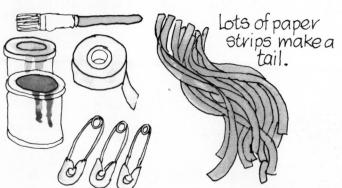

Lots of paper strips make a tail.

Two strong supermarket paper bags make the horse's head. Another bag makes ears, a mane and a tail.

This bag goes on your head.

Cut a look-out hole in each bag.

This bag makes the horse nose

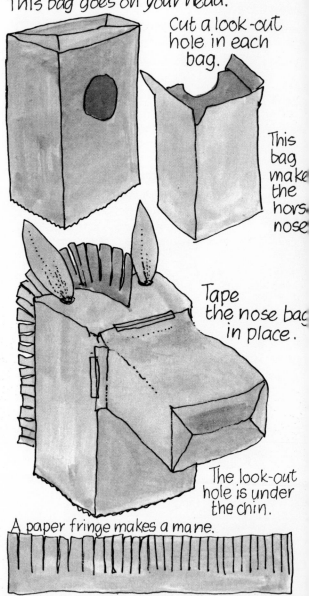

Tape the nose bag in place.

The look-out hole is under the chin.

A paper fringe makes a mane.

Paint the head to match the body.
You should wear horse-coloured trousers
and shoes.

Pants

Baggy pants can be useful. You might need brown ones for the legs of a pantomime horse, or white ones for painting patterns on, or striped ones for pyjamas.

These can be quickly made. Use an old pair of pants that fit you well as a pattern.

You will need a piece of material a bit wider than you and twice as long as your length from waist to ground.

You will also need pins, a needle and thread, chalk and a piece of elastic longer than the size of your waist.

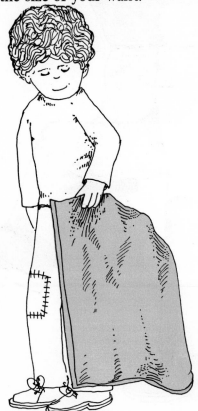

Fold the material in half to make a long thin shape.

Fold your old pants in half— side seam to side seam.

Pin the pants to the material.

Draw a chalk line about 5cm from the pants all around.

Unpin the pants and fold them in half the other way.

Draw around them again.

Cut out the shape you have drawn.

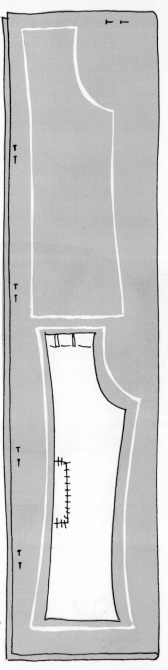

Pin the back leg shapes to the front leg shapes, right sides together. The back legs have the largest curve.

Sew down the sides of each part.

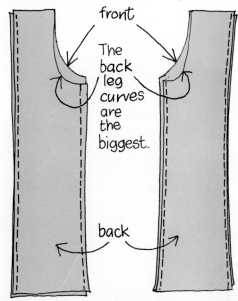

front

The back leg curves are the biggest.

back

Turn one leg right side out and put it inside the other. Make sure the front and back curves are together.

Pin and then sew the curve together like this. An extra row of stitching is a good idea.

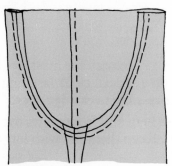

Turn the pants inside out and try them on. You can cut the top of the pants to the level you want them. But leave enough material to fold over for a waistband.

Turn the waistband over and sew nearly all around. Thread the elastic through the waist. A large safety pin on the threading end makes this easier.

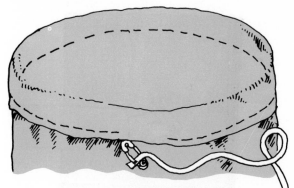

Try the pants on again to test how tight you need the elastic. Cut it off, overlap the ends and sew them together.

Hem the leg bottoms to the length you need – and the pants are finished.

A patch you like can be sewn on.

Cloak

This is a way to make a swirling cloak from a large square of material. A table cloth works well.

Lay your square flat and fold it in half then in half again. Draw a large curve for the hem and a small curve for the neck hole.

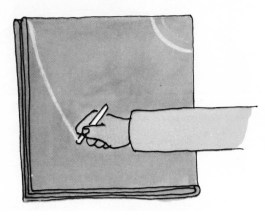

Then cut along your lines. Four thicknesses are hard to cut through so cut the top layer first for a pattern.

Clear a large space on the floor to work on. Open out the circle and lie it flat. Now cut a straight slit from the outside in to the neck hole.

Neat edges aren't necessary for most cloaks, but they will help a special cloak last longer. Use an iron to press the neck edge over.

Fold the bottom hem and front edges over and press them, too. Keep them flat with lots of pins.

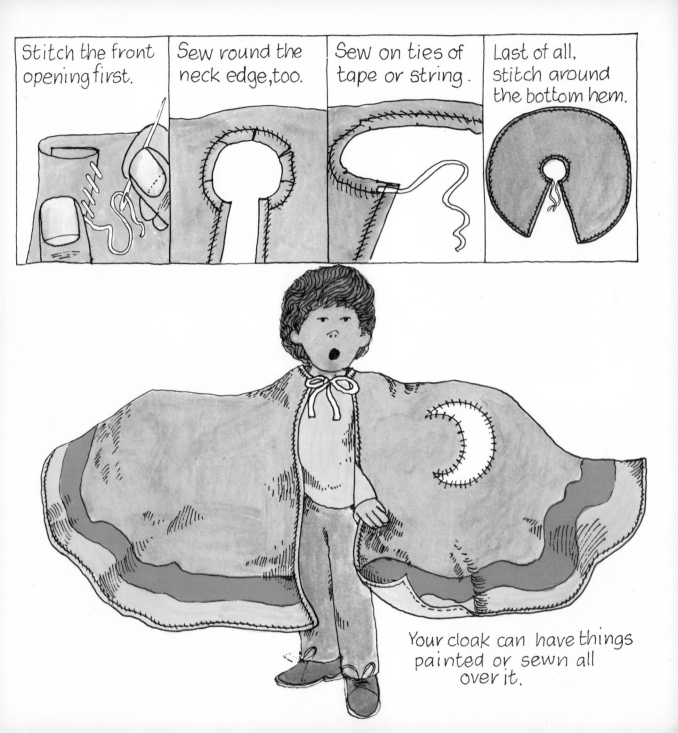

Stitch the front opening first.

Sew round the neck edge, too.

Sew on ties of tape or string.

Last of all, stitch around the bottom hem.

Your cloak can have things painted or sewn all over it.

Bosoms and bottoms

Here are some ways to make large bosoms and bottoms for wearing under your clothes.

They stay in place rather well so you can run and jump in them.

Old stretchy tights are the best things to use. You can stuff them with more tights or with soft rags.

Cut one leg off so you have a long tube.

Stuff it in two lumps and divide them with strings.

Tie them on – or use large safety pins.

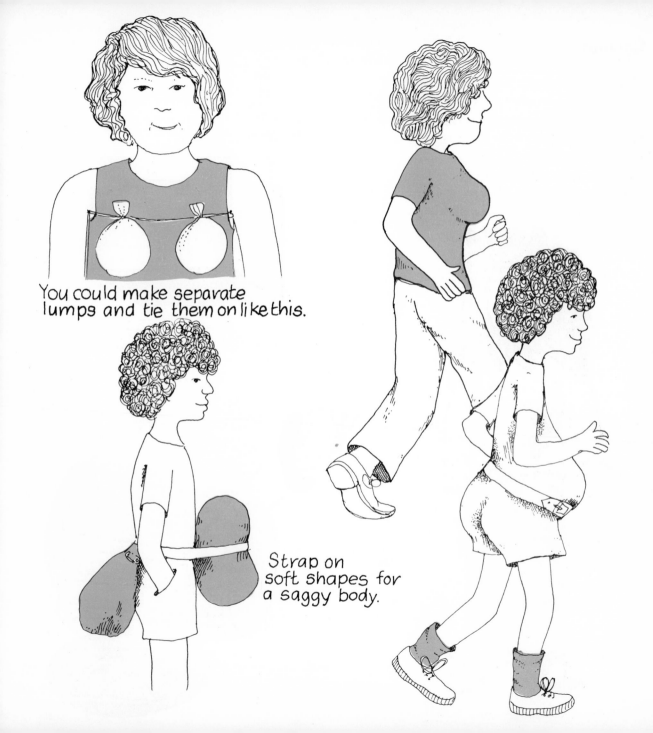

You could make separate lumps and tie them on like this.

Strap on soft shapes for a saggy body.

Camouflage

This means making yourself part of the scenery – so you can't be easily spotted.

In leafy places camouflaging yourself isn't hard. Twist stems into wreaths for your head and shoulders.

Carry a bunch of leaves to cover your face when necessary. Wear green and brown clothes and keep your body hidden in the bushes.

To camouflage yourself in open spaces, wear the disguise of something that might be found there.

Cut a peephole in a box large enough to sit inside. Wrap and label it to look like a parcel.

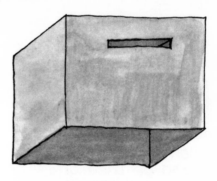

An old garbage bin makes another disguise. Scrub it clean and saw the bottom off. Make a peephole, too.

A wood saw or hacksaw will cut a plastic bin.

Feet

Hot weather feet are best kept bare. That way you grow your own hard horny soles and strong toes.

Make a pair of bare-foot sandals. Wrap long lengths of elastic around your toes and up to your knees. Things you like can be tucked into the straps.

You will need a piece of elastic a bit taller than you for each leg.

Foot binders are worn in some very cold places to keep out frost. You could make binders from lots of long strips torn from an old blanket or sheet.

Wear socks and long trousers. You wind strips around your feet and up over your trouser bottoms to your knees. Then wind down to your feet again and up again.

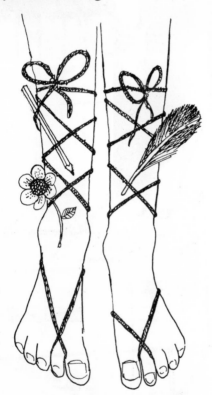

Fold the elastic in half and loop the middle under one toe. Now criss-cross the ends up your leg.

Dry weather boots can be made from long thick socks with cut-out soles sewn on.

Felt or blanket or old overcoat makes strong soles. Thick plastic makes a damp-proof layer. Use wool or string for sewing.

Draw around each foot with felt pen to shape the sole and plastic liner.

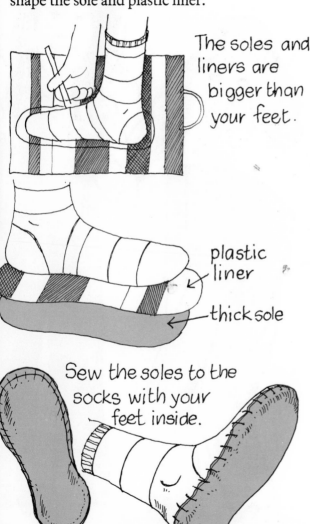

The soles and liners are bigger than your feet.

plastic liner

thick sole

Sew the soles to the socks with your feet inside.

Wear ragged claws sometimes. Make them from a pair of large socks and a white plastic bottle.

Draw claws so the points curve over the bottom of the bottle. They need tabs at the other end to hold them in place.

Cut out enough claws for each foot. Use a sharp knife or scissors for a soft bottle.

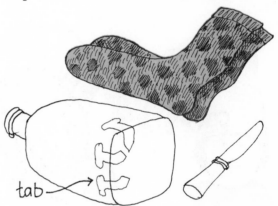

tab

Make small holes in each sock for the claws. Force the pointed ends through from inside. Stuff the toes of the socks with something soft so your foot fits firmly.

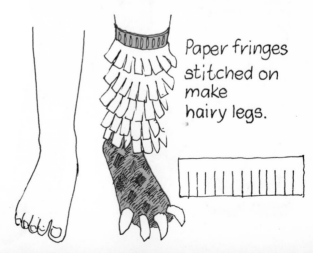

Paper fringes stitched on make hairy legs.

Newspaper hats

Use dozens of sheets of newspaper and hundreds of pins to invent the strangest hats you can.

You could hold a competition with lots of friends – or make a newspaper hat whenever it seems like a good idea.

Change your shape

Make yourself look wider all over. Wear boxes or pillows under your coat. Big shoes and baggy pants make larger legs.

Choose a coat a little smaller than you need and a tiny hat. This makes you look bigger still.

Padded cheeks and small lips painted on make a swollen face.

You can look shorter all over, too. You will need a friend to help.

Kneel down and tie a pair of rubber boots to your knees.

Put your hands on your shoulders and rubber gloves on your elbows for short arms.

Wear a large shirt with sleeves rolled up and a wide hat.

Decorations

Everyday clothes can be made special with decorations sewn or printed on them. You and your friends could make signs for yourselves – or you could make yourself look different from everybody else.

Picture patches can be made from cut-out shapes. Collect scraps of material in lots of colours and patterns.

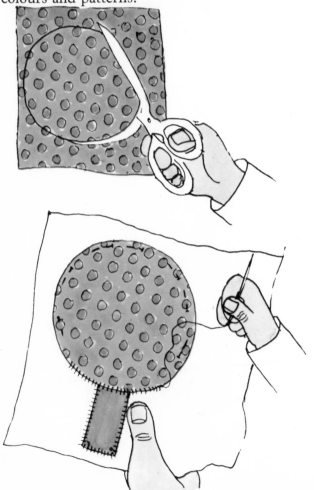

Your initials can go on the pocket of a pair of jeans or on a large patch somewhere.

① Collect buttons of different sizes and colours.

Make paper letters and draw around them on to cloth.

Cover the cloth initials with buttons sewn on.

②

③ Fold over the edges and sew over and over all around.

You can buy special paint for colouring cloth. This stays on in the wash.

For quick results, use felt pens or poster paint on old clothes. You can change your pattern when the first washes out.

Put a plastic bag under the part you are colouring. This stops the paint soaking right through.

A cardboard stencil makes exactly the same shape over and over again.

Use thick paint and a fat brush so the colour can't creep under the edges.

A hand painted T-shirt can tell people something about how you are feeling.

FREEWAYS STINK

Heads

Change your head with a wig. You will need lots of hairy string or thick wool. Any colour looks good.

Wind your string or wool around the back of a kitchen chair. Short pieces can be knotted together.

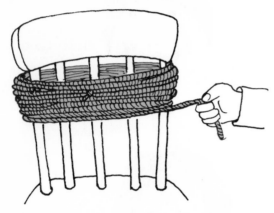

Hold the strands together while you cut through them all in one place.

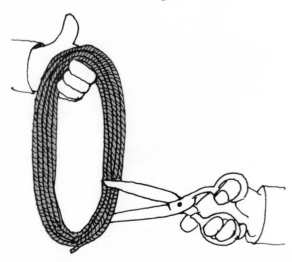

Now take one strand for the centre string. Knot it around a bunch of wool.

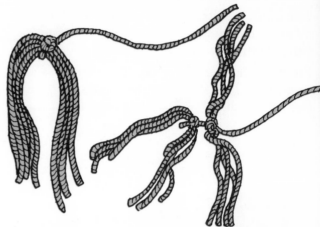

Keep knotting bunches on until you have made a wig to cover your whole head. Push the knots firmly together. Check your back view in a mirror.

Now knot the centre strand to hold the last bunch on.

Trim the wig to suit your face.

You can make a bald-headed wig from the crown of an old hat. Something skin-coloured works best. Straw hats can be painted.

You will need lots of thick wool or string and a large needle. Sew round and round the edge making loops as you go.

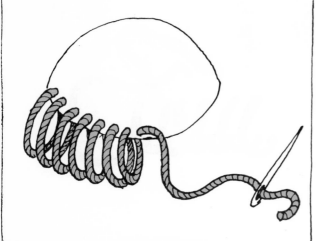

Trim the loops to cover your hair.

Horns can be useful. These horns look as if you've had them all your life.

You will need
an egg carton
2 white candles
some thin elastic

Cut 2 cups from the egg carton and stand them on newspaper.

Melt the candles over a low heat and take out the wicks with a fork. Now wait for the wax to cool down and start to harden again.

Scoop out a handful of wax and shape it into a small curving horn. Quickly mould the horn to the top of the egg carton.

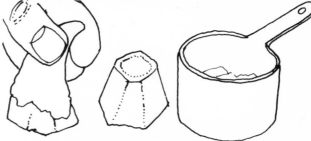

Now coat the sides of the base in wax. If the wax gets too hard melt it again.

Make a second horn. Then coat both horns all over with a smooth layer of wax.

When your horns are quite hard, punch small holes in the sides with a nail. Thread elastic through and tie the horns on firmly.

Blanket coat

This chunky coat fits over lots of clothes to keep out the coldest wind.

The sections of the coat have straight sides to make joining easy. You can change the shapes to suit yourself. Try a floor-length coat, longer sleeves or no sleeves at all.

Old blanket or thick felt are the best materials to use. You will need very sharp scissors to cut the shapes. Find lots of bright coloured knitting wool for the stitching.

You could cut the sections out of paper first to check the fit.

Make one front about 6 cm wider than the other. This gives an overlap for fastening the coat.

Use this stitch for joining 2 pieces.

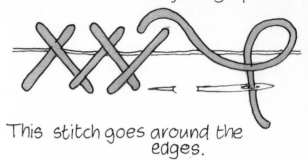

This stitch goes around the edges.

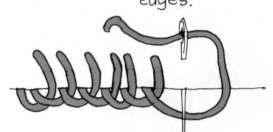

Measure yourself and cut the pieces 5 cm bigger than you are.

Cut 2 square sleeves from a folded edge.

back

2 fronts

1 Spread all the pieces out flat on the floor. Sew the shoulders together and the sleeves to the body. Keep the stitches close together and just tight enough to keep both edges touching.

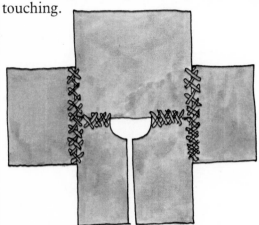

2 Try the coat on and check the length of the sleeves. Cut some off if you like.

Fold the coat over and sew the edges of the sleeves and down the sides of the body.

3 Stitch around all the edges to stop them fraying. Sew at least 1 cm in from the edge for a strong stitch.

4 Sew on tapes or plaits of wool. Stitch them to the edge of the wider front and about 6 cm in from the other edge.

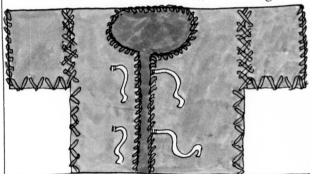

Press the coat with a damp cloth and a hot iron.

Sari

The climate and customs where you live decide what you wear. People all over the world have worked out different ways to cover themselves.

Millions of people dress themselves in long lengths of material. These are draped with such skill they need no fastenings.

Many women in India and Pakistan and Sri Lanka wear saris. They start to wear them when they are about 11 years old.

Saris are often very beautiful. They can be specially woven with embroidered patterns at one end. This end always goes over the left shoulder. A sari is about $4\frac{1}{2}$ metres long and about $1\frac{1}{4}$ metres wide.

Here is how a sari is worn. You will need a very long piece of light material – but a real sari is best of all.

Under a sari you wear a petticoat with a drawstring waistband. The sari is tucked in at the waist. A belt would do if you don't have a petticoat.

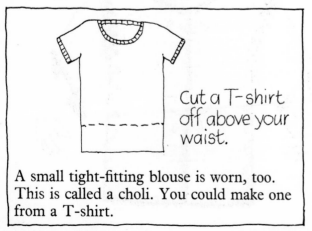

Cut a T-shirt off above your waist.

A small tight-fitting blouse is worn, too. This is called a choli. You could make one from a T-shirt.

① Start at your right side with the plain end of the sari.

Tuck the corner in firmly at the waist.

② Take the sari around you once, tucking in as you go.

Tuck in enough for the sari to hang to your ankles.

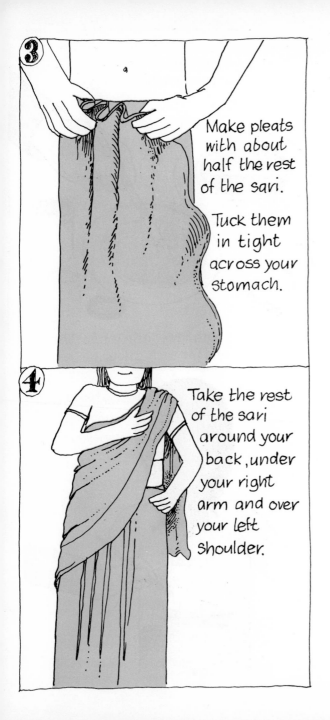

3 Make pleats with about half the rest of the sari.

Tuck them in tight across your stomach.

4 Take the rest of the sari around your back, under your right arm and over your left shoulder.

Saris are worn with lots of bangles. You could make an ankle bell on a chain to wear, too.

Cover your head with the patterned end if the day is hot.

Body paint

Bodies can be painted with non-toxic poster paints. You will need a friend to help.

Some skins don't like some things. Try a patch of paint inside your elbow. If your skins get red or sore, you need another paint. Keep paint away from eyes and mouths, too.

Flour rubbed into hair looks good with body paint.

Cover yourself in cold cream or Vaseline or cooking oil rubbed well into your skin. This stops the paint staining and gives a glossy finish.

Mix the paint with very little water. Use fat brushes – one for each colour.

This body paint never gets really dry – so touch it carefully.

You can use other things for decorating yourself. Charcoal works well. Burn one end of a cork for black markings.

Mud can be found in many colours for body paint. Watch for rich-coloured muds and collect them in jars. Mud can be kept for a long time.

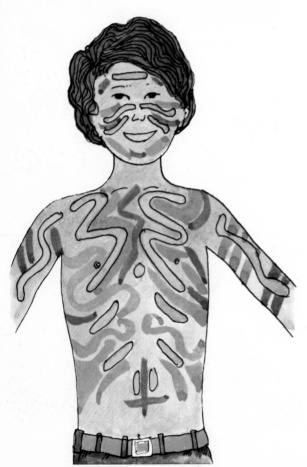

Just mix in a little water when you want to paint. Poster paint can be added to mud for stronger colours.

Lumpy skin can be made from things around the house.

Cornflakes and breadcrumbs make putty for rashes. Tissues soaked in honey make scars. Colour them to match your skin. Corn syrup holds them in place.

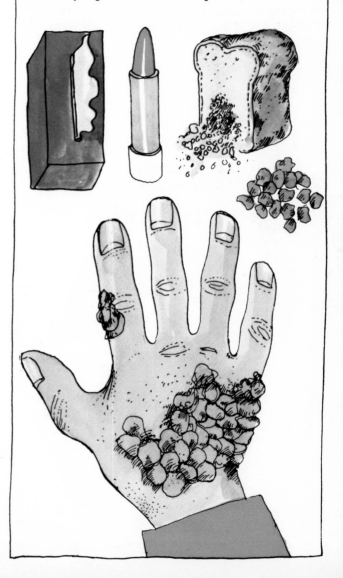

Wet weather gear

Most raincoats you buy take up a lot of space. This means you often don't have them when you need them.

Here are two ways to keep rain out with large plastic garbage bags. They cost very little and fold up small enough to fit in a pocket or a bike pack.

A simple cape can be made by just pushing one of a bag's closed corners into the other. This is what farmers often do with sacks if they are caught in a storm.

Tie a piece of string under your chin to keep the hood on in the wind.

A longer-lasting cape can be made from the very strong bags people use for garden rubbish. They are made to hold twigs so they don't tear easily.

Cut an opening up the middle. Short slits each side in the closed end make a neck hole.

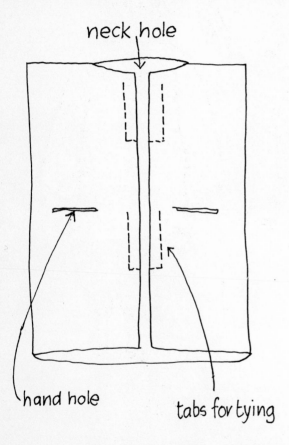

neck hole

hand hole

tabs for tying

Cut 4 short fat tabs in the front edges to tie the cape shut.

Try on your cape and mark where you want hand holes. Make them wider than your arms so you have room to move.

Tail

A tail is a surprising thing to have. Make a long droopy one. Hang it through a hole cut in the seat of an old pair of jeans.

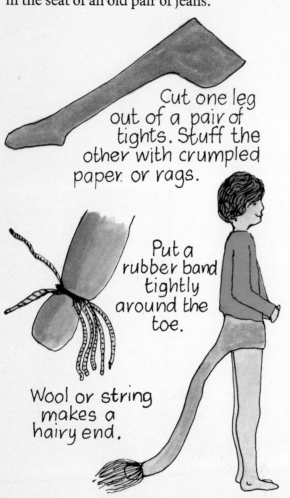

Cut one leg out of a pair of tights. Stuff the other with crumpled paper or rags.

Put a rubber band tightly around the toe.

Wool or string makes a hairy end.

Cut a hole in the trouser seam just big enough to push the tail through.

Practise walking and sitting in your tail so it becomes part of you.